Faking No More

eying the veil

Manoj Mahendru

BookLeaf Publishing

India | USA | UK

To YogMartand SatGurunath Siddhanath,
who honed my testing blade of reason into a
feathered heart that hums the unstruck one
in two veils. In seven spirals I unwounded
with his subtle transmissions, deluded with
His unconditional love for humanity,
culminating my twenty-five years of a silent
quest. Now my soul's compass turns inward,
and in this hush, I bow wordfully.

YogMartand SatGurunath Siddhanath

My essence, my SatGurunath, the only life-breath-giving Sage of the Himalayas, who has shattered all the shackles that once held me in the iron clutches of labels. Sharing His breath, He infuses me with life as He does with all who breathe the breath of love, beyond the walls of caste, creed, and all the illusions that divide.

Dedication to "The Curtain Raider"

— The transformative experience of my Master, YogMartand SatGurunath Siddhanath, "Rudravtara."

Upon Himalayan heights, where snowy summits gleam,

A truth-seeker embarked, following a mystic dream.

Yogiraj, heart aflame, tread a path of yore,

Guided by Nath Masters' wisdom, forevermore.

Through emerald valleys, where pine-scented breezes sigh,

He heard echoes of ancients, beneath an endless sky.

Raja Sundernath, with locks like moonlit snow,

Stood sentinel of truth, where eternal rivers flow.

A maiden, eyes aglow, became his gentle guide,

To a cavern of secrets, where mystic songs reside.

In the depths of the mountain, bathed in golden light,

He saw the Presence in a bright vision before him—Shiva—

Goraksha-Babaji.

A symphony of light and sound, dance of cosmic grace,

Expanded his consciousness upon that endless, most holy space.

Gentle implosions, like waves upon the sand,

Erased the ego's hold and the Promised Land.

Within the embrace of unity, all one and whole in oneness,

He beheld within himself the divine: source for every soul.

A call to love and service, to heal and mend,

With spirit soaring free, his journey did transcend.

Anew he wandered forth, a beacon of light,

Ancient wisdom taught by his calm and Presence bright.

In every breath and step, the divine he'd trace,

Tender-graceful in love and knowledge through space.

Acknowledgments

To my wife Deepika, my son Heramb, my brother Vikram, and my parents—thank you for enduring my delightful nonsense with the patience of saints and the occasional eye-roll. Your support has been the sturdy raft navigating the wild currents of my paradoxical, self-imposed solitude on the path lovingly carved (and occasionally chuckled at by all) by my master, YogMartand SatGurunath Siddhanath. Truly, I couldn't have trudged this trail without your confused yet unwavering presence.

Preface

Faking No More— a prequel to Faking Humanity No More

In the twilight on a mindless cup of tea, we now enter a realm where illusions fade away and the old gods of imitation scatter like startled birds. We have lived the costume of "Faking Spirituality" and watched its soul settle in moist eyes. We have lifted the veil of "Faking Reality" dissolving its mirages in soils of intellect. Now, the third and most tender unveiling begins with the prequel "Faking No More." Here, masks drop completely, leaving us basking in a sunlight so colorless that it both warms and warns.

Before you proceed, know this: These words do not solely arise from my own heart. They are guided by the unseen hand of my beloved spiritual master, YogMartand SatGurunath Siddhanath, who hums softly in the recesses of my stillness. His presence infuses these phrases with deeper "that-is" and through his untiring blessing, the pen dances across this page. To him I bow, for his wisdom makes this path possible.

Like a mischievous sage whispering cosmic punchlines, I invite you further into these shining corridors of perception. Can you smell the incense of cherished beliefs burning on the altar of wakefulness? Tread gently, traveler, for with each chapter some comforting crutch crumbles beneath your feet. You wobble between laughter and tears, between sorrow's melodic ache and the humming emptiness beyond all names and forms.

Here, you encounter only yourself—yet who are you really? Is humanity a brittle shell or a cosmic seed, awaiting wings? Let us strip away all disguises until only laughter and radiant silence remain.

Manoj Mahendru

The Reality Swap

Hopping between one and two,
I wonder why I am "me" and "you".
I still myself oft, but I create tasks,
And I know I am fed up with all masks.
When would I become Who All is,
When I am myself with all that is.-

May It Be

Pierced by That which pierces all, we dig and
rise,
in one heart's deep, where all care resides,
disguised—
not maybe, maybe not, terms twist and
cleave,
desire kisses desire, yet deceives.

Inside the void's own void, we act the trace,
of soul in soul's own longing to embrace.
Maybe to be, or maybe not—yet clear,
it's That within, both near and nowhere near.

God Particle

In a wider universe, that speck takes part,
Hidden in its dance, both the end and the
start.
Like shadows on stone, that ancients would
tell,
Its mystery deepens and holds us in its spell.

Is it a wave? Is it a dot? Both stories it tells,
A question, a puzzle, where relative theory
dwells.
Is it all of what's real, or just scholars' tales?
Its true guise, perhaps, behind the veils it
conceals.

Among the vast stars and the stretch of time's
thread,
It starts its own jig, and onward it's led.
Though our eyes try to catch and hold it in
sight,
It murmurs, "Not today, and not this very
night."

Like grains that elude when grasped in the
hand,
Its truths remain distant, hard to understand.
But its rhythm, its pulse, in our soul does stay,
For in its enigmatic dance, we find our own
way.

Another Pilgrimage

Another pilgrimage bends time's breath,
Laying whispers on the river's skin.
Eternity spirals where moments cleave—
Love's gravity warps what never begins.

The wave collapses in the karmic sweep,
Particles scatter, then gather to bind.
Pulse of the infinite hums in retreat,
Tracing the circle where spirit unwinds.

Telepathy

The body shivers with labored breath,
The doctor's mind, in knowledge, kept.
The healer, pained in ego's pride,
While sickness in the genes hides.

From skies beyond, the ancestors gaze,
Tracing evolution's mystic ways.
The mind tests with tutored lore,
As wisdom calls on the intellect's door.

Who cures, who feels the healing's grace?
Illusion voids the heart's deep place.
The limbs, in wild motion thrown,
While rest, lost in impulses, unknown.

One reflection aware of ancient weight,
May cleanse the sins that bind our fate.
A pause, mirrored deep within,
Fulfills the last rites of spiritual kin.

Mind relapse

The skin of time slips—
Nij, you call it, your own, but whose? A mask
stitched with days,
Nasvar, fading under each touch, every
breath,
But Amar laughs, standing still, waiting in
the shadow of your blink,
Anjan, a smear of clarity across the brow, or
is it the heart?

Truth flickers, then hides—
Nath watches, not the puppet of this fleeting
world,
But the master of its dance,
A spin of eternity on the tip of a perishing
toe,
While you chase the echo, he holds the silence
between steps,
Anjan shines, not to see, but to know.

The Weaver

In the streams of Pran, where the subtle
glides,
The Chetan mind of the holy Presence tides,
Where thought's frail skin on spirit's sea doth
ride,
And breath becomes the thread by which we
bide.

O Nath, unweaver of the woven veil,
Whose light doth stitch the tapestry with a
cosmic nail,
You undo the knots on duality's well-knit
tale,
And crown the soul in the One, where
universes prevail.

Soul fire

My heart burns
with the soul of unburnt desires,
honoring the undying love
of settled thoughts.

The tides of my breath
still the moons that shine
through the darkness of my fears.

I dig through the ethereal sand
of my earthly existence,
and find myself flowing
with the humors
the Spirit plays within us.

Allakh

The Lightless burst of a thousand hopes,
A belief shining through veils and robes.
Born with the spark that ends all illusion,
Why should I mind the darkness of doubtful
passion?

In my errands, I forget the battles I know,
Yet my breath clings to what is restfully true.
How do storms strangle my ancient fires?
Only when I choke my air under desires.

Exert Not

"More, more, more," they say,
forgetting the power of being.

We're born with courage,
like trees in a storm,
finding strength in the struggle.

Our minds love labels,
but under all the noise,
there's a quiet truth we know.

Dreams don't need magic,
just small steps every day,
satisfaction in the journey.

The world can be harsh,
but your light, my friend,
was never meant to be hidden.

In quiet moments,
when you're not trying so hard,
you'll see you're already shining.

The Karma Mile

1.

in midnight's maze
fate's thread knots tight
pulp fictions pulse
under the mean night

2.

Withered streets shadow
echo steps we've traced
karma's tireless ways
swift, with suspenseful grace

3.

Like scarred heroes, fallen
walk their destined path
karma, ever patient and watchful
deals its righteous wrath

4.

lives unfurl, unmasking
truths under mind's veil
actions multiply, karma's
hand will never fail.

Back Home

let yourself go
and sink softly
into the tender
divine soul
wisdom (where healing
wears out
the mind's worn
weight)

(in this
inward
motion)
a natural
decline soothes,
you must
clear out
and free
yourself from advances
unnecessary.

let go, let others
test their power,
responsibility (while

you
step back
to allow
the divinely
tested ending)

give yourself some time,
space, let be,
just be,
let the soul's calm
method
provide
a promised
healing
process
meant for
you.

cherish this chance
to expand
your vocabulary
of emotion
and let the divine
(guide you home)

The Living Book

In actions, lies the destiny of our fate,
Intentions pure, a freedom to create.
Karma, not a book with a spine,
But a living story, yours and mine.

Endeavour with calm, an effortless thread,
Beyond the routine of life and death.
In peace, we strive; in faith, we soar,
Transcending realms every now, evermore.

In striving calmly, minds transcend death's
hold,
For we bear God's image, stories yet untold.
Faith's radiant embrace grants immortality,
Where karmic bonds dissolve in pure
tranquility.

As Above, So it is

In my soul's quiet,
Echoes of mystic mind resound,
Life's journey is a magic fable,
A lesson we delight in unlearning.

Reality cradles my heart in a serene embrace,
Reason's voice is but a treacherous thunder,
In my darkest hours, my thoughts murmur,
Experiencing self-acceptance without none.

From adversity's deep wisdom,
I hear the silence of the Self,
Where in stillness, the Universe secrets tell,
A dance of inner calm, silence surrenders too.

The quest for true joy,
What lies above is tended below,
Gossips and truths overlapped,
As above, so it is,
In the stillness, I endure.

Fake it to make it

Sadness lingers, spirits low,
Joy feels distant, doesn't flow.
But fake a smile, laugh out loud,
Happiness will come, I vow.

Even when your heart feels glum,
Let your mind pretend it's fun.
Act as if you're filled with glee,
And soon that joy will set you free.

So fool yourself; it's not a crime,
Just play along; it works just fine.
Fake it till you make it; that's the key,
Happiness will follow, you'll see.

I am That

Radiant sun, your might I embody,
Illuminating all that exists to be.
I am the Vedas' essence, eternally free,
An intimate vision for all to lifefully see.

My subtle sound, a Pranava flame,
Resounds like a bell's soulful ring.
Brahman's realization is my true aim,
As Adityavarna, all sounds I sing.

Echoes

Honey, ain't no running from the echo of your
deeds,
Reason's just a whisper in a house of broken
creeds.
You think your thoughts are angels, but they
are demons in disguise,
Born from reason's womb, wearing truth's
alibis.

You do the thing; it leaves a tough mark,
Like a stain on your favorite shirt, can't hide
it in the dark.
Thoughts in your head, they come around,
Whispers of the choices you wish you hadn't
owned.

So own it, dude, head high, no blame,
Flash a smile; let love lead the game.

Two paths

Two paths in life we tread each day,
Seeking gain in every way.
We breathe and lose in a cycle so tight,
Chasing quick pleasures, missing what's right.
Ledgers we love, true profits ignored,
In routines we're trapped, actions implored.
Society guides us, sets the norm,
Backward we move, despite the reform.
Far is our goal, the journey we love,
Updating our maps, the route we shove.
Why do we stick to the well-worn trail,

Failing ourselves when missions derail?
All we desire is peace everlasting,
Yet prestige we seek, the effort outlasting.
Our minds drive us to give and take,
Ego's desires we rarely forsake.
True self we find when we surrender,
Acting freely, seeing Divine splendor.

The Self-Worth loop

Behind the veil, where actions stand, not just
a hand,
Mind's a fortress, heart's land, where true
selves are planned.
Freedom's gift, the realest proof, not for your
own booth,
Self-worth ain't in thought's loop but in the
truth's troop.

The last fight

Against fate's flow, your passion's sharp, a
blade in the night,
Cutting through despair, your faith stands
tall, so right.
As the curtain drops on this epic journey,
you're the quest's best,
In love's wild play, you're the guest, in your
final test, bringing light.

In the twilight of your battle, fraught with
ardor and strife,
Your heart, a defiant warrior, seeks the solace
of love's fief.
Against the tide of fate, you wield your
passion as a knife,
Carving a path through despair, a testament
to belief.

Reflection

Mirror, mirror, on the wall,
Why does my image seem so small?
Opinions grow stronger every day,
In a mind's maze, I've lost my way.

Alone

Alone in my days and dreams,
How do I unfeel the love I hold?
Truth expresses not in what seems,
Heart throbs in silence, aloof and cold.

Alone
During my days and in my dreams,
How can I not feel the love I hold?
Truth is not evident in how it seems,
My heart beats quietly, distant and cold.

Zeroing In-Out

In the Sutras, The Wise One says,
"Let go of the mind and see through the haze,
Seedless desire—nothing to hold, just
pure awareness, no stories told."
But what's this balance, I hear you ask?
Sahaja's the art of doing no task, as
spontaneity flows like fire in streams,
while the Equal-You sits, steady in walking
dreams.
One hand's in the sky, the other in the soil,
both
clap together, come what may.
A joke from the cosmos; it seems quite an act
without stretching, yet reach the sky.
So here's it, no seed, no grind,
Stillness' the state of tricking the mind.
Laugh as you fall on the bridge so thin,
You've already won—by not trying to win!

योगशाला

श्री हरिवंश राय बच्चन रचित मधुशाला से प्रेरित और मेरे
प्रिय सतगुरु, योगमर्तंड सतगुरुनाथ सिद्धनाथ, को
समर्पित जिन्होंने साँच हाला को मुझ चित पान कराया ॥

नाथालय जाने को घर से,
चलता है इक मतवाला ।
बंधन उसका पीछा ना छोड़े,
असमंजस में है भोला भाला ॥
मन रोक रहा उसको लेकिन,
दिल उसको बतलाता है।
साश्वत सत्य पाना है तो चला चल योगशाला ॥

कई दिल बीते चल-चल के,
पर पिरो ना पाया साँसों की माला ।
इक डोर खींची जाये उसे सदियों से
वो फिरे लेके अरमानों का प्याला ।
          कई बार ज़म ज़म से तृप्त हुआ,
          कई गंगाजल श्नान किए।
          प्यास उठी फिर सत्गुरु की
          आब-ओ-हयात में तैर पहुँचा
योगशाला।

मैंपन का पथ सरल था
जिसपे चल अस्थिर हुई मारुत ज्वाला
मन दूर निकल चुका था देह से
देख ना पाया पैरों का इक भी छाला।
          लाउडस्पीकर बुला रहे थे,
          मंदिर गूंजे घंटों से,
          कान चीख रहे थे क्षोभ में
          पर आँखों में चमक उठी योगशाला ।

रुद्राक्ष पहन लिए गले में
पर ख़ाली था नैनों का प्याला ।
समय को क़ैद किया मोह जाल में
किस डोरी में पिरोता साँसों की माला ।
          सुबह निकल लेता हूँ घर से
          कमाने ख़ुशियों की रोटियाँ।

भर नहीं पाया उस भूख को
जिसको तृप्त करेगी तो योगशाला ।

आज चला हूँ सब आडंबर छोड़.
उस अहम को त्याग जिसे जन्मों से सम्भाला।
साँस फूल रही है पथ कठिन है,
कैसा है माया का जंजाला।
धर्म ग्रंथ सब छोड़ दिये अब,
जिनका भार उठाये चलते सब ।
पुरुषार्थ को प्राणों में खींच,
ढूँढा फिरूँ मैं योगशाला।

जला डाले सब मोह के बंधन,
ठंडा कर दिया क्रोध विकराला ।
वहाँ चला हूँ जहाँ,
ना छाए अंधेरा ना चमके उजाला ।
साँस फूलती हैं तो रुकता हूँ,
समेट लेता हूँ उसे मुट्ठी में.
यही मेरा जीवन सरमाया,
जिसे अर्पण करूँ जा योगशाला।

महक रहा सब अंदर बाहर,
जैसे सुगंधित गौशाला ।
मेरी देह मेरी बांसुरी,
जिसे बजाऊँ बन प्रेमी ग्वाला ।

कैसा संगीत बज उठा,
जिसकी सुगंध करम भस्म करे।
रहूँगा विचलित फिर भी मैं,
जब तक ना महकाये योगशाला ।

कैसे बना दिन रात हर पल
यह करमों का मकड़ जाला ।
कभी लॉजिक के दांतों से काटा।
कभी पकड़ा भक्ति का भाला।
कैसी चाल चली क़िस्मत ने,
कि क़िस्मत को बदल दिया।
अब सब छोड़ बहा जाता हूँ,
उस छोर जहां सिर्फ़ योगशाला ।

किसने बदला भाग्य को,
कौन था वो क़िस्मतवाला।
इस मैंपन से मैंपन भस्म किया,
ले प्रज्वलित साँसों की ज्वाला।
इक ज्वालामुखी जलती है अंदर,
जो ठंडा कर देगी "मैं अग्नि" को,
सब खो जाने वालों के,
भाग्य चमकाती योगशाला।

किसी रूह ने लिखी रूबाइयत,
कोई लिख गया मधुशाला।

इक रोशनी की तलाश में,
कितनों ने काग़ज़ किया काला।
क्या सीखा किसी ने अब तक,
सब ने दिल को समझ से समझा।
कई रात ना सोये मतवाले,
वो ही सुबह को पहुँचे योगशाला।

मदिरालय का रस्ता पकड़ा,
थक के तोड़ा साक़ी का प्याला।
क्या बल था उस मदिरा में,
मतवाला बन ना सका लतवाला ।
धर्मों के चक्कर भी ऐसे थे,
जो भटकाना जानते थे।
भटक-भटक के सीख गया,
अंतर भ्रमण कराये योगशाला ।

मन के बंधन बहुत जटिल हैं
तन से कर्म करता जाये करनेवाला।
जन्मों से जाल बुने चला जाता है
कुंजी लिए ढूँढे दिल का ताला।
ओंकार गूँजे गगन मण्डल में।
जिसका क्षितिज बसे अंत करण में।
कर्मस्थल का कालचक्र तोड़
नया युग सजाये योगशाला।

प्राण और मन त्त्व को ले के चला
पिया चेतन प्राण का हलाहल हाला।
ध्यान से मन को चैतन्य-शांत किया
और प्राणत्मा को किया आनंद-शिवाला ।
         बहुत दूर नहीं पहुँचा अभी,
         रुकूँ तो मन ठहरता ही नहीं।
         अपनी प्रेम अनुभूति को रक्त किए,
         प्रवाह करूँ जा योगशाला ।

जीत हार अंतर्द्वंद ग्रीष्म गहन
जीत कर भी हारा जीतनेवाला ।
प्रेमभाव से करने चला मन शुद्ध
जीवन लीला की चित्तशाला।
         द्वैत अद्वैत का विनिमय खेल
         कब तक चित्त व्याकुल करे।
         स्थिर प्राण किए चला जाऊँ मैं
         रस्ता भी ख़ुद बनी योगशाला।

मंदिर मस्जिद हैं असमंजस में
कैसे लगायें मेरे दिल को ताला ।
मेरे कदम कैसे रुकें किताबों से
जब मेरे सत्य ने जलायी हर पाठशाला ।
         छोड़ गये सब बोलने वाले
         मेरा सत्य कुछ ना कह पाया।
         सब फूँकने वाले कैसे जाने

कैसे शून्य-प्रज्वलित योगशाला।

अनुभूति का बाजूबंद शृंगार किए,
श्रद्धा के फूलों की पहनी माला।
सदभाव का धन संजोऊँ पल-पल मैं
निकला लोभ व्यवसाय का दिवाला।
कठिनाइयों के काँटे थक गये
जब सुख के आतिशों पर जन्मों चला।
संसार के गोरखधंधे भस्म हुए
जब गोरख अलख बन गई योगशाला
।

कब कल्कि आयेंगे धारा पे
कब रोशन होगा शंभाला।
हर पल कलियुग सतयुग गुज़रे
करमों ने ऐसा काला जादू डाला।
सत्गुरु को पाया प्रभु रूप में
मन का क्रिया अनुराग किया
क्या समझायें पंडित मौलवी मुझे
जो पा ना सके अंतर योगशाला

To be continued in the sequel...

Me in Enemy

O my envy enemy,
why you envy my soul,
You know, I nap in your mind,
And Your envy rests your ennui.

Your enemy mind calls You,
To end the animosity,
Of your sleep and rest,
In one memory of wisdom.

Wise your "I" in your true eye,
And mirror your "self" in your mind,
You will not find yourself,

I reside there wisefully.

Wake up!!

The Curious Case of Soulful Mind

In mind where rivers flow up so high,
And silent birds shout to the sky.
The sun dips east, the moon kisses morn,
Night snores loudly, stars stretch and yawn.

In darkness, where gravity unwinds,
A tiny black hole bright light finds.
Hear the silence of glowing white,
Taste the echoes of colors bright.

So scratch your head and ponder deep,
In this illusion, where senses sleep.
For upside-down is right-side right,
When a reverse river fills your sight.

What stories do the ears impart,
When eyes listen and minds depart?
Who scolds the judge so cold and calm,
How to bear the sting of soul's balm.

Illogical coherence
Coherent Expansion

Beneath the mandala of the infinite,
where stars, sharp as shards of frozen time,
scatter their scars across spacetime's weave—
a story webs, not bound by arrhythmic
rhyme;
by the torrents of knowing in unknowing.

Einstein tilts the axe of perception,
a soft bending of time into the lap of gravity.
Moments stretch, contract—a comic truth
that bends to mass, to light, to the darker
edges
of a dimension we dare to map but never
own.

Hawking peeps behind the eye-lit veil,
where the dark hums with the memory of
radiance.
Black holes, not monsters, but thresholds—
their silence doors fragments of existence,
a flinch of decay and renewal, unyielding,
infinite.

Bohr steps into the smallest of the Ghost,
where particles dupe between being and
becoming,
where uncertainty whispers its laws—
a wave, a particle, a maybe blinded into That.
The cosmos, it seems, thrives on irony.

Oppenheimer holds fire in his palm,
not as a destroyer, but as a witness
to the alchemy of life's endless upheaval.
From the atom's quiet rage, a phoenix rises,
ash and genesis braided into one breath.

Kabir's voice cuts like a scythe,
sharp and rustic, he sings of the space
between opposites—where the drop

becomes the sea, and the sea
gathers itself back into the drop.

Sage Siddhanath interplays "out-inward",
Through the wire of breath, of silent verbs.
Under his flight, the void is a mirror,

and in the mirror, all swans sing their lifeful
death
Deathful life, the self, mere ripples in a
parody.

Here lies the quantum emergence:
not in answers, but in the discrete interplay,
where light and dark swap places,
where time is neither for nor back,
but always turns into the eternal now.

O wanderer, there is no one destination,
only this dual moment, this unraveling,
this endless weaving of two into one,
and one to two, the loom of subtle connect
unsilent in the soul cry.

चुभन

हो सकता है या हो सकता नहीं,
चुभता वही जो सबको चुभता वहीं।
दिल की गहराई में हम मन खो जाते,
जहाँ हर चिंता छुपी है, सुख पाते।

चाह की चाह में, कुछ तो छल जाए,
इच्छा से मिलके इच्छा फिर बल जाए।
शून्य के शून्य में, हम बिंद चिह्न बनाएँ,
आत्मा से आत्मा के मिलन की राह पाएँ।

होना न होना, ये प्रश्न हमेशा,
वो ही पास है जो दूर ही रहता।

Ouroboros

In spine's bind, I wound round freedom's
thread,
Released from wayward breath's maze
run;
A self unmade where thoughts lay shed,
In void's quiet pulse, all selves shun.

Fault lines

In the bated breath, the chaos unfolds,
beyond the veils, where evils dissolve—
alchemy hums, not in gold,
but in the blur where the two resolve.

Common Sense

The senses whirl my mind's frail compass off,
its whirlwind—casting waves that flood each
thought.
Yet faith, that Bethlehem of stillness, "stars",
me true, as I unname these intimate storms.
I dim the din to silence, where lights fade,
My colorless will senses calm's clear path.

The Butcher

Kabir says I reside near
my shadow choker
Are you my enemy I awe?
When you are so kind
eyeing my neck now and then
I think I am your God
As you embrace your mind in me.

The Curious Case of Soulful Mind

In mind where rivers flow up so high,
And silent birds shout to the sky.
The sun dips east, the moon kisses morn,
Night snores loudly, stars stretch and yawn.

In darkness, where gravity unwinds,
A tiny black hole bright light finds.
Hear the silence of glowing white,
Taste the echoes of colors bright.

So scratch your head and ponder deep,
In this illusion, where senses sleep.
For upside-down is right-side right,
When a reverse river fills your sight.

What stories do the ears impart,
When eyes listen and minds depart?
Who scolds the judge so cold and calm,
How to bear the sting of soul's balm.

Vice and Versa.

The duality of
a kind, and more—
Is the will of That
which is The One.
It keeps me in unrest
in the lingo of keepsakes.
My will or His stance—
the gap, my dear friend.
I stand as adversary
yet fault finds me.
The bridge stands
my ego, senseless.
I stretch out in empathy
stretch inward in ego.
Vice and verse pin
my verses to the vices.

The clouds vibrate
my impulses throb.
I control the Source
in the motor of my senses.
Oh, to be the thunderbolt

that stills the sky.
My belief in "what is"
waits still
for what should be.

The New Will

That spark of will-power
That is immortal
Is you.
That hand of hope
That is real
Is you.
That act of serendipity
That is nursed
Is you.
That breath of courage
That is steady
Is you.
That bridge of faith
That never falters

Is you.
That whisper in the silence
That speaks truth
Is you.
That flicker in the darkness
That guides the lost
Is you.
That seed of resilience
That blooms in adversity
Is you.
That heart of compassion
That beats for others
Is you.
You are That.

I overslept

I was sleeping in another night, but then your
dream
Made me sleepless, into a trance extreme.
The old colors looked cool, but your day is
bolder,
A whole new reality, like a love shoulder.

Echoing the taught did me no good,
You roar the anthem, understood?
You've nursed the guts, the sky's-the-limit
view,
The kind of hands God gives to a chosen few.

Now I chase the lost, I never found,
Retracing the fears, break new ground.
The old dream must nap, your star is born,

Together, we're unstoppable, that's for damn
sure.

See the Seer

In twilight's grasp, the seer dissolves into air,
Where sight and seer become a boundless sea,
Worlds beyond the mortal stare he'll share,
Living truths where only the soul can see.

Whirling visions fill the trance-like mist,
Consciousness and void become one;
The silent witness, in surrender, kissed,
Fades into that eternally luminous sun.

Barter

In the trade of life, if resistance had no role to
play,
Wouldn't the Beloved be but a smile away?
If in the pursuit of force, night and day I
waste,
How then the heart's true rest I taste?
This portal of love, rusted by the dull
mindscape,

Oh, had I but bartered smiles and sighs like
those who escape.
Now, my heart a closet in the market of
longing, ablaze,
Donating pressures to reject or attain, for His
desireful gaze.
In the loss of existence, with my all I stand,
Praying the Beloved wins me with a generous
hand.

#AliveYouAre

When many fake the best of their minds,
Face the tempest in all its might.
You are moving on day and night,
Some burdens more and indeed more less,
Enduring some, leaving rest for tomorrow.
When you ripe, you might miss to see,
How many hills you climb with your ease.
The one you earned with your steps,
The ease nobody dares to question.
I know you are questioned well,
Less by others and more by your patterns.
But I know you tricked all tests,
The last day when you chose to endure.

NOne

When the two become one-to-end duality,
And all zeroes add to forge the infinity of
Reality.
Who wants to walk or who desires to reach?
Everything and anything has only Nothing to
teach.

Being Personal

In the mirror of the Existence, I wear no
sheet,
Amidst shadows and light, I am a real person
at least.
I accept no adjectives; in the depth, I
immerse,
A soul in the play, living in the Reality-verse.

The Equilibrium

In the heart of the city, where lights dazzle
and glow,
A dreamer seeks truths as he wanders to and
fro.
Amidst the chaos, he seeks the divine and the
sacred,
Yearning for his heart to soar, free and
undeterred.

Mastering the art of letting go, without
abandoning love's flow,
Balancing between worldly joys and the inner
glow.
With the grace of an acrobat on a tightrope
line,
He finds his equal in life's rhythm divine.
The metropolis teaches through its
labyrinthine streets,
In its locked paths, the art of release it
repeats.
Though at times the spirit may falter and feel
alone,
Through all trials, the sun's warm rays are ever
your own.

Dustless

In life's bustling bazaar so bright,
Timeless bound for what catches sight.
If it shines, it's sold, I swirl and spin,
Yet, within, the soul's light grows dim.
Eyes drawn to glitter, I chase the fame,
Losing sight of heart, in this wayward game.
Insta allure, my heart's vision misled,
Audiobook of my face, left unsaid.
Irony stands, in the shadow's swell,
Tweeting to be seen, yet deep within I fell.
Blind to my Self, in display I trust,
Lost in the shine, my essence turns to dust.

Urban Views: When Shadows Pass

1. In Alleys Dark and Deep
In the backstreets where memories seep,
Graffiti on walls, whispering "This too shall pass."
Shadows of old fights, of wounds, of wrath,
Yet morning lulls them asleep.

2. Metro Hustle
Amidst the rush, a tear, a scathed hush,
A missed train, a breakup, seems like life's crash.
But tracks go on, so does the song's bass,
For every tunnel's end, there's a hopeful flash.

3. Skyline Stories
Buildings high, playing the sky,
Housing tales of heartbreak, loss, impasse.
Yet the skyline changes; old towers crumble, new ones amass,
The homeless one echoing again: "This too shall pass."

4. At the Café Corner
Sips of coffee, whiffs of past romance,
Bitter taste of failure, of a missed-call class.
But flavors evolve, sweet memories in a glass,
With spine's brew, even the bitterest
moments pass.

5. Park Benches, Night Glances
Lovers' quarrels, sarcastic stances,
Under the moon's ever-watchful brass.
Yet with dawn's first ray, the Satan doesn't
last,
New beginnings, new chances, a new Trust.

6. Downtown Melodies
In the heart of the city, amidst horns and
dance,
A songstress laments of love, of contrast.
But as notes ascend, sorrows won't outlast,
For in music, she finds: "This too shall pass."

7. Rooftop Reverie
Above it all, where steps amass,
Gazing at stars, contemplating the impasse.

The silent whispers, breaking the hourglass,
With divine miracle, no challenge trespass.

8. Rain Over Potholes
Water fills, as car tires splash,
Puddles reflecting pains, mistakes en masse.
But rain also cleanses, as seasons transgress,
Offering hope's umbrella: "This too shall pass."

9. City's Heartbeat at Dawn
As the sun parches the urban morass,
Fresh starts arise from yesterday's overpass.
For in every tick and every tock's brass,
Someone resounds life's promise: "This too
shall pass."